T0125117

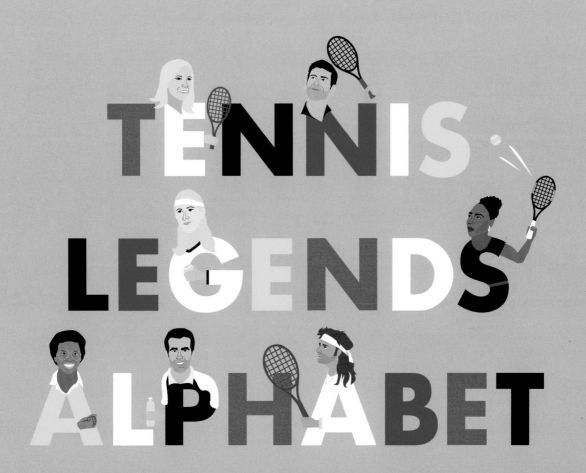

TENNIS LEGENDS ALPHABET

Words by Robin Feiner

A is for **A**ndre Agassi. Brash newcomer turned role model, Agassi retired an eight-time Grand Slam title champ and Olympic gold medalist. 'The greatest returner in the game' now pours his energy into charity work for disadvantaged kids.

B is for **Bj**örn Borg.
This teenage sensation went on to set the tennis world on fire in the 1970s, becoming the first man to win 11 Grand Slam titles and over a million dollars in prize money in a single season! 'Ice Man' was voted Sweden's most legendary sportsperson of all time.

Cc

C is for Jimmy Connors.
A fiery ball of energy
and determination, no one
gave their all like 'Jimbo.'
As reward for his efforts,
he won eight majors and,
in 2019, still holds the record
for number of titles won in
the Open Era (109). Legend!

D is for Don Budge.
In 1938, this popular American became the first player in history to complete the Grand Slam in one year, a monumental feat that took 25 years to equal. This gentleman of the game was considered the 'complete package' and one of the greatest ever.

E is for Chris **E**vert. Bursting onto the scene at the age of 16, the 'Ice Maiden' soon shot to No. 1 and became the game's most influential role model. Her composed baseline style and signature double-handed backhand bagged a legendary 18 majors in singles and three in doubles.

F is for Roger **F**ederer. With his poetic game and gentlemanly demeanor, the Swiss maestro is celebrated as one of the greatest legends the game has ever seen. With 20 Grand Slam singles titles to his name, he also won the tour Sportsmanship Award a staggering 13 times. All hail, King Roger!

G is for Steffi Graf.
With her athletic ability
and aggressive game at the
baseline, Graf is credited with
inventing the modern style.
As well as winning 22 Grand
Slam titles, Germany's golden
girl made history as the first
and only winner of a Golden
Grand Slam. Wunderbar!

H is for Martina **H**ingis. Setting records as the youngest Grand Slam champion and youngest World No. 1, her strategic mind made her brilliant at singles and even better at doubles. Hingis was appointed the first Global Ambassador for the Tennis Hall of Fame.

I is for Ivan Lendl. While he never won Wimbledon, the Czech with the big serve and lethal top-spin forehand dominated tennis in the 1980s. He brought a quiet, steely focus to the game, and transformed the sport with his systematic approach to training.

J is for John McEnroe.
This controversial fireball
is possibly the most infamous
player in tennis history!
His unique mix of talent,
temper and outright
competitiveness made his
matches truly unforgettable.
His rivalry with Björn Borg
is just legendary.

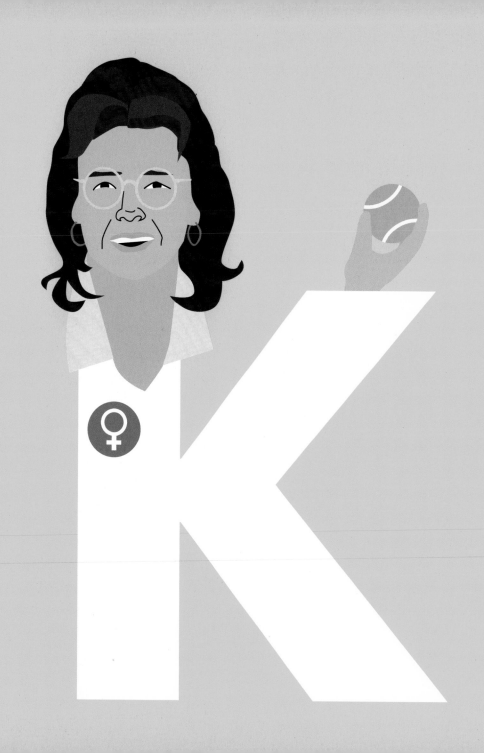

Kk

K is for Billie Jean King. Small, speedy and aggressive, this outspoken revolutionary refused to conform from the get-go, appearing in a junior group photo wearing shorts instead of a skirt. With 39 major titles to her name, she fought for and won gender equality for women in tennis.

L is for Rod Laver.
Finalists of the Australian
Open play on Rod Laver Arena.
That's because 'Rocket'–
the left-handed Aussie with
a record 200 singles titles
(amateur and Open Era) and
two calendar-year Grand
Slams – is considered one
of the greatest legends in
the history of the sport!

M is for **M**artina Navratilova. She was hitting a tennis ball against a concrete wall in Prague at the age of four, and had won the Czechoslovakian national tennis title by age 15. Including doubles, she won more Grand Slam titles than any other player in history!

N is for **N**ovak Djokovic. The man with the most singles Grand Slam wins, and the only player to complete the career Golden Masters, 'Joker' also holds a non-calendar year Grand Slam! He's been hailed as one of the greats by fellow legends like Rod Laver, and is said to be the most 'perfect player of all time.'

Oo

O is for Mary Ewing Outerbridge. After falling in love with tennis while living in Bermuda, Mary brought the game back with her to the U.S. in 1874. She set up a court on Staten Island and played the first match against her sister. Mary was inducted into the International Tennis Hall of Fame in 1981.

P is for **P**ete Sampras. With his deadly serve, 'Pistol Pete' was World No.1 for six consecutive years. His 14 Grand Slam titles – seven at Wimbledon – was a record at the time. His epic battles against Andre Agassi in the 1990s were legendary!

Q is for Adrian **Q**uist. During the 1930s and 40s, this Aussie showed the world how doubles were meant to be played. He was the doubles champion at the Australian Open 10 consecutive times, and also won a Career Grand Slam in doubles. What a legendary team player.

R is for **R**afael Nadal. This jumping, fist-pumping, bicep-bearing Spaniard thrills audiences with his intense will to win. Now, with French Open Championships into the double-digits, 'Rafa' is the 'King of Clay' and one of the greatest of all time.

Ss

S is for Monica **S**eles. Unconventional double-handed strokes saw this vibrant 16-year-old become the youngest-ever French Open winner. She went on to bag nine Grand Slam titles, inventing the tennis grunt along the way. Sadly, she was prevented from realizing her full potential.

T is for Bill **T**ilden.
As World No. 1 for six years,
he dominated the world of
international tennis in the first
half of the 1920s. During his
18-year amateur period,
'Big Bill' won a staggering
138 of 192 tournaments,
and was the first American
male to win Wimbledon.

U is for **U**mpire Carlos Ramos. This Portuguese gold badge chair umpire is the only man to have presided over all four Grand Slam tournament finals, as well as the Olympics. Very few players dare trifle with the steely nerve of Ramos!

V is for **V**enus Williams. With seven Grand Slam singles titles and 14 in doubles – all with her sister Serena – Venus is a champion celebrated for her power and athleticism. This former World No. 1 can also proudly boast four Olympic gold medals.

Ww

W is for Serena **Williams**. With her sister Venus, Serena is credited with ushering in a new era of power and athleticism in women's tennis. With 23 Grand Slam singles titles – a record in the Open Era – Serena retired arguably the greatest female player in tennis history.

X is for Arant**x**a Sánchez Vicario. Crowned ITF World Champion in 1994, the 'Barcelona Bumblebee' was renowned for chasing down every last point! While she was a fierce singles player, she was devastating on the doubles court with 10 Grand Slam doubles titles to her name.

Yy

Y is for **Y**annick Noah.
He skyrocketed to hero status in 1983 when he became the first Frenchman in 37 years to win the French Open! He was inducted into the International Tennis Hall of Fame in 2005, and now captains France's Davis Cup and Fed Cup teams.

Zz

Z is for **Z**suzsa Körmöczy. The year 1958 was a big one for this Hungarian legend. At the age of 34, Zsuzsa won the French Championships and reached the semi-finals at Wimbledon. She was named Hungarian Sportswoman of the Year, and in 2007, inducted into the International Jewish Sports Hall of Fame.

The ever-expanding legendary library

EXPLORE THESE LEGENDARY ALPHABETS & MORE AT WWW.ALPHABETLEGENDS.COM

TENNIS LEGENDS ALPHABET - 2ND EDITION
www.alphabetlegends.com

Published by Alphabet Legends Pty Ltd in 2023
Created by Beck Feiner
Copyright © Alphabet Legends Pty Ltd 2023

9 780648 506300